Effective Communication Skills:

How to Enjoy Conversations, Build Assertiveness,
& Have Great Interactions for Meaningful
Relationships

Keith Coleman

Table of Contents

>>GET A FREE & EXCLUSIVE SELF-DISCIPLINE COPY<<

To instantly download **a free copy of Self-Discipline** – "5 powerful steps to refill motivation and practice self-control" **not available elsewhere**,

Visit: **http://bit.ly/displin**

Introduction

Imagine a life where you are the ultimate people magnet who wields a powerful influence over people. How about being a person who has people eating out of their hands? Or a person who can hold people spellbound with their conversation skills? Imagine being a person who has people hanging on to every word you utter or actively seek your company. Imagine having an unspoken hold, control and influence over people. The power to persuade people to do anything you want them to. The power to form beneficial, fulfilling and gratifying social relationships that help you meet your objectives. This is the master key that has the power to unlock your destiny – the ability to connect with people.

What if I told you can be all this and more. Yes, you can. Wherever you are currently on the social skills quotient or meter, you can be a social skills champ through consistency and effort. With the right intention, you will not just survive social relationships and situations but conquer them.

Social intelligence can be described as a person's proficiency in social skills, proficiency, and behavior. Some colloquial terms that best describe social intelligence are street smartness or common sense. This intelligence type is distinct from the intelligence evaluated through IQ tests. Social intelligence is generally affected by the environment. Communication skills are vital for having sound social intelligence.

The ability to effectively communicate with people in multiple situations and settings indicates social intelligence and proficiency. Behaving efficiently in social situations is vital to one's personal and professional success.

Social intelligence correlates with emotional intelligence is the sense that it is crucial to read other people's emotions, and experience empathy for others. Social intelligence is a highly developed and acquired skill that can be enhanced by a person taking action and actively working on their emotional and social intelligence.

If you ask me the number one skill for success in today's world, it is the relationship and rapport building. Irrespective of your technical skills, cognitive intelligence, and experience, success in today's people-driven world boils down to your ability to connect with people and form rewarding social relationships.

If you don't identify as someone who wields this sort of magnetism on people, you aren't alone. Plenty of people around the world are socially awkward or face varying degrees of social anxiety. They are worried about not being interesting enough for others or probably not being able to say the right things at the right time.

They think they are being judged all the time for not being good enough or people laugh at them behind their back. They may not be confident or self-assured in social situations. They experience physiological anxiety symptoms such as sweating, increased palpitations, rapid heartbeat and so on in varying degrees in a majority of social situations.

One of the biggest challenges people with low social intelligence grapple with is their inability to connect with or relate to people. When interacting with an individual or a group of people, they don't believe they 'belong' there. There is a tendency to feel disconnected and out of place among people.

On the other hand, people with high social intelligence are able to connect with people almost effortlessly or at least able to make it seem effortless. They don't have a hard time gathering more emotional and psychological information about the person and then optimize this invaluable resource to form highly fulfilling relationships.

If you identify more or less with this, you have company. I've got your back here. Several people are sailing in the same boat as you. They are petrified of social situations or feel they like a complete mess when faced with the prospect of initiating conversations or responding to people. There's an overwhelming feeling of never saying or doing anything right in a social situation.

This book is designed to hold your hand and take you through the step by step process of transforming from a socially awkward to a socially coveted and hugely popular individual. It'll help you gain the confidence to move up the social ladder, form fulfilling relationships, and meet your objectives.

Building and negotiating social relationships has multiple benefits. You'll lead a less stressful life, enjoy greater positivity around you, meet your personal and professional goals, spread goodness around you, and inspire people to do well, and achieve wealth, success and good fortune.

Typical signs of social intelligence include -

Effective speaking and listening skills – A socially adept or intelligent person doesn't merely listen without reacting or preparing a response. They actively listen to understand and empathize with what the other person says. Each time you speak to a socially intelligent individual, you'll walk away thinking that you were heard and understood. You'll go with the feeling that you've connected with someone and not merely spoken to them.

Brilliant conversation skills – Socially intelligent people will completely capture your attention, imagination, and interest in their enthralling conversation skills. They possess an inherent or carefully cultivated gift of the gab that allows them to hold people's attention through their words. They will say the right things at the right time, and will always have people clamoring to them for their negotiation skills, tactfulness, humor, sincerity, and meaningfulness. Heard about people who have the power to 'work the room?' They are the ones!

These are people who are earnest while expressing themselves, can recall minute details about others and create a thoroughly meaningful and captivating dialogue. Don't worry if you don't identify with this. I didn't either at one point in my life. However, this is my reality today. You can go from being a rock who finds it virtually impossible to respond and relate to people, to a people's person who loves being surrounded by others. It isn't easy, but it's doable.

<u>Socially intelligent people rarely argue</u> - People with high social intelligence will rarely argue to prove their point. They perceive the need to prove your point as pointless. Socially intelligent people will rarely attack other people's emotions or hurt them in a bid to prove themselves right. They will seldom squash other people's views and ideas.

These people listen to everyone with an open mind and are able to appreciate other people's need to disagree. They possess the empathy to understand where the other person is coming from, and why they think the way they do even if they don't necessarily agree with them. They agree to disagree respectfully rather than having a "my way or the highway stance." They are accommodating and mindful of other's people's needs, desires, views, and preferences.

Socially intelligent people are better at reputation management – Socially intelligent people are conscious of the impression they leave over others. Reputation management requires more than just ace conversation skills or negotiation power. It is a complicated attribute of social intelligence that requires a mix of being genuine or true to one's nature and creating a stellar impression on other people. Reputation management involves sweeping people off their feet while staying authentic.

Social intelligence isn't the simplest skill to master. However, it's not impossible either. Once you master it using a series of solid, actionable tips mentioned in this book, you'll seldom be tongue-tied at a party or not know how to respond articulately when someone you've only just met initiates a conversation for the first time. You'll lead a more fulfilling, socially richer life, build more harmonious professional relationships, open doors to plenty of opportunities through networking and make new friends.

The idea is to be proactive about changing your situation from a socially awkward or shy person to a social star. The change begins with a strong desire to be a socially confident person. You must realize there is a challenge, and feel a compelling desire to overcome this challenge. There must be an overpowering need to enjoy and master social relationships.

People with high social intelligence display nourishing and healthy behavior, which makes people around them feel important and valued. They have mastered the art of making others feel good (make that great) about themselves. They will make feel loved, appreciated, inspired and respected. They have a distinct appeal and are described as demonstrating a magnetic personality.

On the contrary, people with low social intelligence are toxic, and generally, have a negative effect on people. They make others feel devalued, disrespected, guilty, frustrated, angry or inferior. They end up alienating people. Some people are unintentional and unknowingly toxic, owing it to their reduced social intelligence. At times, they unintentionally say the wrong thing and end up hurting people or making them feel not so good about themselves.

At times, without realizing we may keep sending negative vibes to people through our words and actions. Socially inept people are so preoccupied with their stress that they overlook the effect of their behavior on other people. They undergo drastic behavior or personality changes when they are made to realize how others perceive them.

The best part about social intelligence is it can be improved. Not everyone is blessed with remarkable social skills. However, everyone has a good chance of increasing their social intelligence. Unlike, cognitive intelligence, which is more or less fixed and impacted by genetics, social intelligence can be nurtured and developed over a period of time. Throughout the book, I am sharing my best kept and most valuable pieces of actionable advice about mastering social relationships by being an effective communicator.

Several psychologists and sociologists are of the view that social intelligence should be a development priority during childhood, teen years, and the adult professional world. Socially intelligent people are successful in the art of influencing others to accomplish their objectives, demonstrating empathy and winning the respect of others. It is more than simply making yourself likable! Being high on social intelligence is about minimizing conflict, building effective collaboration, and ensuring common goals and the greater good is efficiently met.

Harvard professor, Howard Gardner, first put forth the theory of multiple intelligence or intelligence other than cognitive intelligence. Human intelligence, according to Gardner, comprises multiple interwoven competencies or intelligence.

These are broadly classified are practical intelligence, kinesthetic intelligence, emotional intelligence, aesthetic intelligence, and social intelligence. Think of this intelligence as varied dimensions of a cube, each placed at a distinct angle with others but combing together to complete the whole. They are different pieces of a puzzle that come together to complete the picture.

Successful people boast of a combination of multiple intelligences. Their intelligence is more comprehensive and integrated, though there's never an ideal. The idea of multiple intelligences suggests that these abilities are things people can master or enhance in their adulthood.

Social intelligence takes hard work, practice, and effort. Start by giving more attention to the social world surrounding you. Consciously work on becoming a more effective speaker, listener, and conversationalist. Networking organizations, speaking groups, public speaking classes can help you develop effective communication skills. Actively work on becoming an effective listener. It is also about working on your verbal and non-verbal people analyzing skills. Being socially intelligent is an aggregation of skills that involves understanding people and making them feel good about themselves at the basic level. In short, it can be termed "people management."

Why is social intelligence important in the workplace? There is a need to understand the consequences of your behavior on other employees. If you have to lead people, you need to understand what drives and inspires them.

Socio-emotional connection helps retain employees, boost their productivity, and make them feel valued within the organization. A workforce is about team players, not solo acts. When we understand people's emotions and key drivers, it is easier to relate to them. This may not an inborn trait, but evolves over a period of times based on your experiences and interactions with people.

Consider a scenario where two candidates with equal technical or cognitive intelligence, experience, skills, and capabilities are applying for the same position. With all other attributes being the same, if one of them is an ace communicator, can put across his/her views effectively, relates to another - in short, is adept in the art of 'people management' is likelier to get the job than someone who struggles with people management.

Communication forms the cornerstone of all our personal and professional relationships. Mastery of social intelligence is important for everything from acing a job interview to building a powerful network of contacts to earning a date with your crush.

Every relationship we share on this planet is determined by our ability to relate to people. We can't meet our goals ourselves. Seeking help from people, and relating to them needs effective communication.

Neuroscience has found that our brains are designed to be sociable, drawn into a personal brain to brain connection where we engage with other people. Our brains are wired to connect with people at an evolutionary level. This natural bridge influences the brain and body of people we communicate with, just as they influence us. The more we connect with a person emotionally, the higher is the mutual force we experience.

If you need to succeed and are not living under a rock, you need social intelligence to survive and thrive. You need to be able to relate to people and help them relate to you to get them to do what you want them to.

Chapter One:

Small Talk and Rapport Building Secrets

Don't we all know that one person who slays it like a boss when it comes to connecting with people? He/she knows exactly what and how to say things to captivate people's attention. It's almost like they never say or do anything wrong in a social situation. The person is the cynosure of all attention and activity at parties and other social gatherings. What is the secret of being the ultimate people magnet that these people know and others don't? They don't have access to some magic potion that others don't. Chances are they've carefully studied and mastered the art of establishing a rapport with people through small talk. Small talk is fairly big when it comes to striking a rapport with people, and connecting with them at a deeper, subconscious level.

Research has revealed that when we meet people for the first time, it takes us merely 4 seconds to form an impression about them, which more or less remains the same throughout our subsequent encounters with them. Imagine 4 seconds only!

Scary? Maybe Doable? Absolutely! By learning the rules of creating a power-packed first impression and mastering small-talk, you can create the desired first impression. The idea is to make people feel like they belong, to make them feel at ease in your presence and to make your initial interaction unforgettable.

Studies conducted at the Michigan University revealed that small talk and meaningful interactions boost our problem-solving skills. Positive and meaningful communication involves accessing other people's minds and thinking about things from their point of view. This is important when it comes to assessing a problem from various angles and arriving at a solution. It helps us develop strategic thinking, lateral thinking, and problem-solving abilities.

Did you ever wonder how some folks always manage to make plenty of friends, grab free drinks, make memorable conversations and sweep everyone off their feet! The answer is stellar small-talk. Small talk is crucial when it comes to making a positive first impression, and getting people interested in you.

Yet, it is one of the biggest challenges for people with low social intelligence. They break into a sweat when it comes to approaching others for interaction or initiating small talk. The fact that this is your only opportunity to make or break a positive impression adds to the stress. Small talk is the basis of every rewarding personal, professional and social relationship. We form deeper, mutually beneficial and meaningful relationships based on a positive first impression or small-talk.

The goal of small talk is to demonstrate how interesting, knowledgeable and well-informed you are as a person. It is also about rapport-building and identifying a common ground (background, hobbies, lifestyles, desires, fears, goals, aspirations) to support your interactions.

By engaging in small talk, you will be successful in determining if the person is worthy of future interactions for enjoying a more meaningful and beneficial personal, professional and social relationship. Sometimes, informal small-talk can help create lasting relationships with people who are like you or in the same situation as you.

Dazzle people by creating a glowing first impression using these 17 incredibly valuable small talk strategies.

1. Stick to safe, neutral topics – When you are engaging in small talk with a person for the first time (or the first few times), as a thumb rule, stick to neutral, universal, non-controversial and evergreen topics. This holds even more weight when you are communicating with people of different nationalities, cultures, languages, and races. Topics like environment, food, movies, books, city, health, science and technology are relatively safe compared to terrorism, war, and international conflicts.

Identify common interest grounds, and stick to them. For instance, if you realize that the other person is a passionate foodie, stick to topics of new restaurants in town, popular cuisine, global delicacies and so on. Again, if you realize someone is a huge sports fan, discuss weekend games, the best places for sports buffs to visit in and around the city and game strategies. I'll bet my last cent the person will be all pumped up to engage in a positive, energetic and spirited manner.

Several luxury car salespersons are trained in the art of peeking inside their prospective customer's vehicles to pick clues for building conversation and leaving a favorable first impression. For instance, if they find gym gear in the car, they will talk about their own weight or cardio training routine, muscle building strategies and eating right. The objective of this strategy is to increase the salesperson's likeability, build a favorable rapport, and create a phenomenal first impression on the potential customer, which increases the chances of them making a purchase.

2. Look at the newspapers for substance – This is my favorite tips when it comes to mastering small talk at any gathering where I am likely to meet a lot of people for the first time. Before attending the event, take a few minutes to browse the internet or newspapers for the most talked about the latest news. I call it creating a 'conversation bank.' You have matter ready for conversing with people instead of being tongue-tied.

Again, ensure that you don't pick controversial topics. Avoid news related to politics and global conflict, and instead go with safe topics like path scientific research, breakthroughs in health or technological advances, where there is minimal scope for disagreement. Keeping a 'conversation bank' ready handy ensures that there aren't too many clumsy silences and meaningless fillers. This will help you keep the other person hooked.

3. Mirroring is the key – Mirroring is the key to establishing a favorable rapport with another person at a subconscious level. It has existed since primitive times, and throughout evolution. Our brains are wired to recognize and be drawn toward people who seem 'like us.' We instantly take to people who appear similar to us at a subconscious level.

One of the best ways to make someone feel you are like them on a subconscious level without them even realizing it is by mirroring their actions. If you want to strike a positive rapport with someone you've only just met, mirror their body language, gestures, posture, movements, words, voice and so on. Observe their verbal and non-verbal clues and mirror it to establish a feeling of familiarity and belongingness.

A pro-tip here is to keep it subtle to avoid offending the person or giving the impression that you are mimicking/mocking him or her.

Using this technique, you lead people to believe that you are 'one of them' or similar to them. This boosts your likeability quotient and helps you build a positive rapport with just about anyone.

Notice typical words and phrases people use, and use the same words and phrases while conversing with them. For example, if a person refers to their enterprise as "my empire," refer to it as "your empire" each time you talk about their business. On a subconscious level, this boosts your chances of getting the other person to like you and relate to you at a deeper level, thus creating a positive first impression.

The mirroring should be natural and effortless, not forced. Don't appear nervous or like you are making a great effort to follow everything they are doing. It's counterproductive to the idea of being 'like them.' This doesn't just increase your personal appeal, but also helps the other person relate to you more effectively. Individuals will relate and respond to you more positively when you present yourself as someone who they can identify with.

4. Disagree respectfully – During your small talk, you may disagree with what the other person is saying. However, disagree respectfully and healthily without becoming defensive, offensive or confrontational. You will ruin your chances of leaving a favorable impression on the other person. Utilize a diplomatic yet authentic approach like, "this is a new, unique and interesting way of considering things. Can you please elaborate on it?" It is about revealing your disagreement without making the situation unpleasant.

5. Ask more open-ended questions – The secret to knowing more about people, having a flowing conversation, and getting them to open up is to ask more open-ended questions. They won't just end up revealing more about themselves, but also helps you detect a common platform for building the conversation. Avoid making it a one-way interaction. Don't appear like an FBI officer on duty.

Try to keep a balance between sharing some things of your own and subtly urging the other person to speak by throwing open-ended questions to know more about them, so it seems like a more balanced conversation and less of an interrogation. Let us say, for instance, someone is stoked about the upcoming games at the city/town sports club.

You may start the conversation by referring to the upcoming games, or pick up clues from what the other person said about the scheduled games to ask them why they support a particular team or what made them join or be a part of the particular team. Conversation examples – Person A - "Did you hear about the upcoming games at the local club." You – "Oh yes, everyone's pretty excited about it. I support team XYZ, what about you?" Person A – "Oh, I support team EFG" You- "What makes you support EFG?" Person A – "They have a formidable defense, plus I really like player S." You – "Oh yes, that's true, have you played the game at any point in time?" Person A – "Oh yes, I played for the university and local teams for several years before I quit due to an injury." You – "That is mighty impressive, what were your best winning strategies as a player?"

Do you get the flow? The idea is to build conversation by offering bits of information about yourself and asking the other person questions to facilitate a free-flowing conversation and information sharing.

Master conversationalists are adept in the art of identifying other's passions, interests, and key drivers initially in the conversation to base their entire interaction with it. They identify people's 'hot buttons' and stick to them to make more interesting, relatable (very important) and fulfilling conversation. Seasoned conversationalists are people savvy folks who will establish people's interests early in the interaction and build upon it. For example, if you learn that a person is a travel and adventure buff, you may speak about your own travel experiences or ask them to share theirs. You may talk about your own explorations and encounters with varied cultures. How about asking them about their most unforgettable trip or memorable adventure? This way you are paving the way for an exciting conversation to keep people hooked.

6. Mention their name multiple times – If you've read Dale Carnegie's social skills bible *How to Win Friends and Influence People*, you'll realize that that one of the best tips for winning and influencing people is to remember and use their name multiple times throughout the conversation. In a majority of social instances when we meet a person for the first time, there are speed introductions, lots of unknown faces, and a bunch of names to memorize. A lot of information is thrown back and forth, which means not many people can recall these details later. Use this to your advantage and consciously pay attention to details such as people's names. When you use their names in the conversation or in subsequent interactions, they'll be blown you remember it. Everyone loves the sound of their name.

Practice memorizing people's names. One trick is to keep repeating it once you've been introduced to the other person. For example, "Hi, I am Pete." "Hi Pete, What do you do?" "Hey Pete, Where are you from?" Keep repeating their name subtly a few times without making it sound obvious until it is firmly placed in your long-term memory.

Don't you feel more special and valued when people refer to you by your name? Doesn't it give you an overwhelming sense of importance when you realize that out of several other people they met, someone remembers your name? Doesn't it make the interaction more personal and connected-worthy when you address people by their name? Do not feel awkward about addressing people by their names, even if they've just introduced themselves to you.

Using people's names makes you come across as more likable, relatable and desirable. If you don't get a person's name, it is alright to politely ask them to repeat it instead of addressing them with an incorrect name.

7. Dig for some background research – I have a friend who is the ultimate social magnet and has people eating out of his palms. One of the best tips I picked up from him about small talk involves knowing a little about a person's background before you meet them. This isn't always possible because many times you don't know who will be meeting.

However, when you know for instance that you are meeting XYZ person or a group of people for the first time, dig a little for some background information that can help you strike a more meaningful relationship.

For instance, let us assume you are attending a social gathering that is thronged by people who are musically inclined or love singing. You may have a musically inclined friend with several singer friends and acquaintances at the gathering, which means you know people with a particular passion or interest are likely to attend the event. You can dig a little into knowing more about different musical forms, current Chartbusters and so on. This helps you present yourself as a well-informed, likable and interesting person.

Identify things that resonate with several people or a group, and update your information and understanding about it to have plenty of conversation fodder handy. People you've only just met will be hooked to what you are speaking because they are deeply interested in it.

Sometimes, I play virtual Sherlock Holmes and look for the person on social media networks and other sites. Briefly go through people's profiles on social networks to understand their background, interests, and professional roles. You'll get a good hang of their persona to then connect with them using their interests, passions, favorite teams, popular television series, dislikes and more to keep them captivated throughout the interaction.

Know more about an individual before meeting or interacting with them to offer you a distinct advantage in rapport building. However, safeguard against being judgmental about someone when you obtain prior information against them. This is one of the pitfalls of an otherwise brilliant method. Keep an open and flexible mind, and you'll be fine.

8. Avoid talking about unknown and unfamiliar topics – I know it can be wonderful to have a discussion about interspace communication with a NASA scientist, but it's safer to stick to topics and subjects that you are fairly familiar with when it comes to making a favorable first impression or small talk. The thing is, you are already low on confidence, socially hesitant or suffer from the fear of saying the wrong things. If you go with a topic that you aren't familiar with or where the other person has a clear knowledge edge over you, you end up exhibiting your ignorance, which can lead your confidence to nosedive throughout the interaction. You'll seldom recover from saying something stupid or sounding dumb, thus leaving behind a poor impression.

Having a conversation about various topics is amazing. However, be a little judicious and avoid picking topics you have no clue about. Don't throw half-baked information to impress people, it only ends up revealing your lack of knowledge. Experts can call your bluff.

When a person or people are discussing a topic that you know nothing about, don't bluff your way just to get attention. Instead, use self-depreciating humor to honestly admit how "the only space I know about is the distance between my fridge and bedroom" (for the above example of space communication). It is better to be hailed for your sense of humor than being laughed at for your ignorance. You'll come across as a more authentic, genuine and confident person by laughing at your own weaknesses. Learn to transform your weaknesses into strengths. Lack of information or can be used to make yourself appear honest, entertaining, less clinical/mechanical and a likable/relatable person.

Don't be afraid of laughing at yourself. You won't just come across as unpretentious and honest, but also eliminate the opportunity of others laughing at you or taking a dig at your weaknesses. It'll also boost your confidence by several notches. People are more impressed by quick-witted people who have the confidence to confess their weakness than pretentious people who try to reveal their foolhardiness by communicating half-baked knowledge.

9. Keep it more about the other person than you – Ace conservationists realize that small talk and creating a positive impression on people is more about the other person than you. Make other people the focus of the interaction. However, if you realize that he/she is just as socially awkward or lacks confidence in social situations as much as you, slightly shift focus away from them until they start feeling comfortable.

Few people enjoy listening to a person that goes on and on

about their achievements, superpowers, skills, etc. There is no need to share every bit of your life with a stranger, including details about how your neighborhood cat gave birth to a fresh litter. Focusing on the other person makes you come across as less self-centered and more likable. Use more of "You" than "I" through the interaction. This lets people know you are genuinely keen on learning more about them than speaking about yourself. Demonstrate that you are truly interested in them or keen on listening to what they are saying through verbal and non-verbal clues. This will make you truly irresistible.

10. Maintain a balance between questions and statements – Small talk should be a good mix of questions and statements. If you ask people too many questions to pull them in the conversation, you may appear overtly probing. Likewise, if you make excessive statements, they may not get an opportunity to talk.

Make the interaction more meaningful and balanced by combining questions with statements. Start by making a statement, and add a question at the end of it. For example, "I really enjoyed the ABC movie, although a lot of people felt it was hyped, what's your take on it?" You are giving him/her a glimpse of your opinion, while also offering them an opportunity to express their opinion.

11. **Up your listening skills** – Contrary to what people popularly believe, sound communication is not just about possessing superior speaking skills. It is also about practicing active listening to tune in to what the other person is saying.

Of course, speaking skills are integral to the process of communication. However, if you do not actively listen to a person, you will struggle to connect with the other person by saying the right things. Being a star conversationalist doesn't involve talking until you tire out. It is also about understanding where the other person is coming from and responding suitably to what they speak. Make the person feel relaxed and comfortable in your company.

If you want to make a glowing impression on people, give them undivided attention while they are speaking. Keep your body language open, transparent and responsive. Don't cross your arms and legs, bend your head in the direction of the other person slightly when they are addressing you, always keep your feet pointed in the direction of the speaker.

Offer verbal and nonverbal acknowledgments that you are listening to a person. For instance, nodding heading, saying "aha," "I understand" or "I see where you are coming from." Likewise, paraphrase what the other person said to let them know you heard them and to check your understanding/awareness of the situation. Ask questions to demonstrate your keenness and interest in what the person speaks.

Reach out, and offer encouragement, inspiration, positivity, and affirmation wherever needed. I'll let you in on a secret; almost everyone is working on becoming a more effective speaker. However, effective listeners are as much coveted. Be an open, positive and effective listener, and get people to talk about themselves. There is no way to be interesting without being interested!

12. Look at your surroundings for cues – At times when I seriously do not know what to talk about, and the conversation is approaching a dead end, I look at my immediate surroundings or environment for a clue. It can be a tune playing somewhere or a poster on the wall or even someone's attire. Maybe, something someone just said around you or a brochure lying on the floor. There are cues all around the place. You simply need to look. Keep looking around for clues and select something that is appropriate, relevant, and feel-good to talk about.

It can be the party decorations or food. At times, I am talking about the long queue at the buffet or food counter. Initiate a topic about your immediate surroundings, and check how the person reacts. If they react favorably to what you say, it's a clue they are prepared to talk further about it.

If you are in a new place, talk to a local about their city/town. This is especially handy during business conferences, seminars, and other networking events. Ask locals for recommendations and suggestions on places to visit or eat at. This gets people talking about food, city, culture, neighborhoods, local sports and much more. It can open an entire treasure trove of conversation topics. Everyone loves talking about the place they grew up or currently reside in.

When I am invited to a social gathering when I don't really know many people, I often use conversation starters such as, "How are you connected to the or how do you know the host?" This gets us to identify common ground and begin speaking.

13. Use the 20-second rule – If you get confused about how much to talk and how much to listen while making small talk, follow Dr. Mark Goulston's 20-second rule from his book *Just Listen.* Mark offers a practical and actionable solution that is similar to following the traffic rule. In the first 20 seconds of talking, you are functioning on a green light. The other person listens to you if you make interesting, appropriate and relatable statements.

Only an exceptionally skilled conversationalist can hold the listener's attention beyond 30 seconds without being perceived as dull and chatty. The next 20 seconds are your yellow light signal. You are now stretching beyond the limit. After crossing

40 seconds, you move to red light. Stop now and don't do anything beyond 40 seconds. Though the urge to go on can be irresistible, wind up soon!

14. Seek suggestions and advice – Oscar Wilde hits the hammer on the nail when he said, "we all admire the wisdom of those who come to us for advice." Every person admires the good sense of people who come to them for advice or opinion, which means you should make use of this to establish a favorable rapport. When you approach someone for advice, they'll not just feel great about themselves, but also see you as a person with good taste.

People generally love talking about themselves, their life experiences, knowledge and expertise. Research has revealed that talking about ourselves makes us feel good and stimulates similar hormones as when we eat delectable food, make love or intake drugs. Use this strategy to the max for boosting your knowledge or acquiring new insights or learning new things from other people, while making them feel valued and good about themselves. They'll be left with no option but to like you! If you don't know what to talk about, ask people for opinions, suggestions, and advice.

15. Avoid sharing intimate or personal details early on – While some people take their time to open up, others waste no time in sharing their entire life story with the minutest details with strangers. Drives me nuts at times! I don't want to hear about your difficult childhood or rebellious teen years without even knowing you properly.

Stick to sharing interesting information nuggets about yourself without freaking people out with more intimate and confidential information. Not everyone is on the same plane or comfort level when it comes to sharing intimate information. Everyone has a different threshold where such details are concerned.

Also, sharing intimate details with people you've just been introduced to places you at risk, where you don't know how the information will be utilized by the person. Also, avoid badmouthing other people or gossiping to a person you are barely acquainted with. It paints a poor picture of you. You'll come across as a person who can't be trusted to protect other people's secrets or someone who talks bad behind's people's back.

16. Show empathy and agree to disagree – You may disagree with something a person says while breaking the ice or attempting to make small talk. However, disagree in a polite, respectful and healthy manner. Do not get confrontational, aggressive or defensive. You'll only end up ruining your chances of leaving behind a positive impression. Use a more diplomatic and non-offensive stance such as, "now that's a different way of looking at it" or "this is an interesting viewpoint," or I hadn't seen it this way, can you elaborate on it please?"

Work on your empathy if you want to come across as likable. Master the ability to empathize with others by placing yourself in their shoes to understand why they think or feel the way they do even when you don't agree with them.

When someone says something bad has happened to them or how terrible they are feeling early in the conversation say something such as "I can understand why you feel like this" or "I understand this feeling" or "this must be a terrible situation for you. Trust it will be resolved quickly." It helps the other person feel more comfortable talking to you. Maintain healthy empathy levels without going overboard and weeping truckloads to reveal a concern for the other person.

17. When you are stuck for conversation, here are some questions you can ask the other person to bail you out of a potentially embarrassing situation.

1. How do you know the host? Where did you learn about this event? How did you become a part of this federation? In a nutshell, how did he/she land up there?

2. Which is the last movie you saw in the theaters? What did you enjoy or dislike about the film? Do you think it is worth a

watch?

3. Which are some of the town's/city's best hangouts, watering places, restaurants, cafes, parks and more?

4. Which place are you originally from? Is your hometown far from the current place of residence? How is the weather in your hometown? How is the life in your hometown compared to life in the current place of living? Would you prefer living here or back in your hometown if given a chance? Get a person to talk about their place of origin/birth/hometown if you are looking for a perfect ice-breaker. It creates a fuzzy feeling while triggering positive, feel-good emotions in a person. They will automatically connect these positive feelings and emotions to interactions with you, thus increasing your likeability.

5. Why did you pick this profession or choose to work in this particular sector? Were you always interested in this? How did you develop an interest in this? Would you recommend this career option to others or your children?

6. You remind me of a celebrity whose name I can't recall? Which famous person do people mostly compare you with?

7. Which was the last live concert you went to? How was your experience?

8. Which is your current favorite television show? Why do you enjoy it so much? Which television show or movie is a

reflection of your own life? If given an option to live in the setting of any television show, which one would you pick?

9. Which is your highest priority bucket list item?

10. What's the highlight of your day?

11. What do you enjoy doing in your free time?

12. Which is your favorite sports team?

13. What are your hobbies, interests, and skills?

Chapter Two:

Acing the Language and Speech Game

In the previous chapter, we went through everything you can do to conduct small talk confidently and effectively. Here we'll discuss speech, language and voice skills to grow your charisma, increase your confidence in social situations and leave a positive impression. Are you expressing your views in a positive, persuasive and self-assured manner? Are you a compelling communicator? Are you articulate when it comes to addressing a group of listeners/audience? A good conversation/speech has several attributes. Intonation, inflection, tone, words and more pack more meaning into your overall message to help you put across your point articulately.

Here are some ways to boost your speech and language skills to sweep people off their feet.

1. Build an impressive vocabulary – An articulate communicator with a solid vocabulary is much sought after. People who are able to express themselves with the most appropriate words, phrases and expressions are irresistible.

Work on your vocabulary to enhance your confidence in social situations. Commit to mastering three to four new words every day. People with a rich vocabulary seldom have trouble articulating their views and display greater confidence while talking to people.

The difference between a functional vocabulary and extensive vocabulary can be the difference between a black and white and vivid, colorful picture. Paint a picture with your words to make the conversation more interesting and compelling.

Stay away from redundant words and phrases. Avoid using conversation fillers. Keep your sentences short, crisp and to the point. Do not use the most highfalutin words to flaunt your vocabulary. Instead be an effective communicator by using words that convey your ideas and feelings most appropriately. Less is always more in a conversation. Try to say more by using less yet effective words and phrases.

Think of better and more articulate ways to convey your emotions and ideas, For example, you can say "famished" in place of "very hungry" or "livid" instead of "very angry or upset." Try to convey your ideas using more effective words. Replace redundant words and phrases in your daily conversations. For example, instead of saying, "They said xyz about my looks" say "they commented on my looks." The idea is to make your speech crisper, more articulate and tighter by replacing ineffectual words/phrases with more meaningful expressions. Everyday words and phrases such as "big" can become "gigantic," "massive" or "colossal." Similarly, scared can become "petrified" and "spooked," hungry become "famished" and so on. Consciously think of more effective ways to convey the same meaning.

This practice will make you come across as a more engaging, interesting and vibrant conversationalist. A richer and more power-packed vocabulary lends more character, feelings and sensory experiences to the conversation.

The way to go about it is – Use a diary or notebook for listing new words and phrases you come across each day. You can also randomly pick three new words to learn from the dictionary every day, and try to use it in your speech or conversation. Install 'word a day' applications on your phones to keep enriching your vocabulary. It's a work in progress. You'll never know everything. Even if you believe you have a limited vocabulary or aren't able to hold a conversation because you don't know how best to express yourself, breathe easy. There are plenty of ways to build a powerful vocabulary if you have the initiative.

2. Use inflection for more meaning – There are multiple ways to make your conversation more punchy and

41

effective. One of them is to use the power of inflection. Inflection or intonation adds more value and meaning to the communication. Avoid speaking in a singsong manner if you want people to take you seriously.

Try to vary your tone frequently to avoid sounding like a staccato-sound like a newsreader. If you want to come across as an effective communicator, don't speak in a monotone. Intonation will instill more feeling in your speech. It helps the listener comprehend whether you are asking, requesting, commanding, pronouncing a statement or suggesting something. This reduces miscommunication.

At times, ineffective inflection leads to miscommunication. For example, let us say, you want to request someone to do something or ask them if they are up for it. Now, instead of raising the tone at the end, if you keep it flat it will sound more like a statement. It appears as if you are pronouncing a statement or ordering them to do something instead of checking if they can do something. The difference between the two is – you aren't giving them an option to say no to the former, while in the latter they can refuse.

Make an effort to bring more variety and character in your tone if you want to come across as a compelling communicator. Intonation packs more punch in your words and phrases to communicate the perfect ideas and emotions. At times, even a little inflection can change the entire meaning of a sentence from a harmless suggestion to patronizing or condescending. At times, the tone makes all the difference. Our tone and inflection is pretty much the cause of most communication misunderstandings.

Be mindful of the pitch you employ while speaking. Three fundamental pitches are widely used in regular speech - high, mid and low speech. As an effective communicator, use different pitches to play around with your voice to convey feelings, emotions, and intentions as desired.

I always suggest recording your voice or standing in front of the mirror while speaking when you are working on improving your speech delivery. Narrate a story or talk about any topic extempore, for a minute or two. You'll realize exactly how you sound, and recognize areas of development.

3. Make your sounds and pronunciations more articulate – Actively work on your articulations and sounds if you want to come across as an effective communicator. Master phonetics to sound good, and eliminate the scope for misunderstandings. You'll put across the right appropriation and sounds.

Don't mumble, mutter and speak under the breath. Few things are as unimpressive as someone whose words are barely audible. You will keep repeating yourself multiple times, leading to greater misunderstanding and confusion. Open your mouth loud and clear while talking, so your speech has more clarity. Aspiration of sounds is also important when it comes to increasing your speech clarity. Understand where to stretch and condense sounds. A single letter or similar letters can be used to create several sounds, which you should be aware of while speaking.

For example, "bit" and "beat." While the former has a shorter "I" sound, the latter has a more elongated or stretched "ee" sound. Also "pool" and "pull" are aspirated and pronounced differently, even when "u" and "oo" convey similar sounds. Pronouncing a word differently is crucial if you want to communicate the perfect meaning. When in doubt, go through the pronunciations of words online or using a handy smartphone app while using it.

The same letters can be aspirated differently using different phrases and words. For instance, "th" in "thick" is more aspirated or puffed than the "the" sound in "they" or "the." Like "they" and "day" are pronounced differently even when they sound the same. If pronouncing and articulating specific sounds is challenging, try mouth exercises to make your jaws more flexible. Say tongue twisters loudly to master different sounds and articulations.

4. Emphasize on the correct word – Emphasizing on the correct word is important since it can completely alter the meaning of what you are trying to express or communicate. For example, let us consider a sentence along the lines of, "Did you hit him?" Now if you emphasize on "you," it implies that you are asking the listener, was it you who hit him or was it someone else. Similarly, if you emphasize on "hit," it implies that you are asking the listener if they hit the person or did something else to him/her. Again emphasizing on "him" means you are questioning the other person if they hit the person you both are referring to or did something else. The meaning and implication of the sentence change when you emphasize different words! Emphasize the right word to make all the difference when it comes to being an effective communicator.

5. Be mindful of your rate of speech – Notice how some people speak so fast, you can barely understand what they are trying to say. At times, they speak so slowly that you just can't wait for them to finish. The big rule for communicating your point effectively is to keep a steady, uniform and consistent rate of speech. If you speak too quickly, you may come across as anxious, dramatic, nervous or dominating. The listener may not understand what you are trying to communicate. The message is unfortunately lost.

On the contrary, speaking slowly may make you come across as a boring, uninspiring and drab person. The listener may comprehend what you are trying to convey but may run out of patience waiting endlessly for you to finish. The conversation becomes uninteresting and long-winded. The midway is to speak neither too fast nor too slow. Keen an even rate of speech at around 140-160 words/minute, which is perfect. Anything more than 160 words will be tough for your listener or group of listeners to process!

When you make an important point that should stay with your listeners for long after you've finished saying it, pause to create the right effect maintain silence for a few seconds before heading to the next point. Allow the feeling of what you've just said to sink in.

Chapter Three:

Be A Charismatic Conversationalist and Increase Your Social Charisma

Yesteryear Hollywood icon Marilyn Monroe once had a photographer accompany her to New York City's Grand Central Station during the peak hour. The station was predictably crowded with commuters. However, no one awarded her a second glimpse or even recognized her for the star she was. Marilyn boarded a train and traveled to the next station without so much as being noticed. She traveled inconspicuously as Norma Jean (Marilyn's real name). On arriving at the crowded NYC streets, she dropped her average person guard within seconds, puffed up her mane, and took on a hypnotic pose (she was an expert at it, we all know).

In a few seconds and strokes of genius, plain Jane Norma Jean transformed into the star Marilyn Monroe! The onlookers were enchanted by her presence. What was it that made her go from humdrum to bedazzling? She was gorgeous of course. However, there was something unputdownable at work that increased her mojo! This X factor can be termed charisma.

One of the best aspects of charisma is, it isn't an inborn trait. Most celebrities and public figures work hard on it. We all have a Marilyn Monroe within us, waiting to reveal her true charisma.

How can you build an irresistible social persona or magnetic social power? What are the traits that differentiate ace communicators from regular ones? What are the unspoken, hidden x-factors that reality show judges look for in contestants?

Tap into your hidden star with these awesome tips to boost your social charisma. Trust me; every Norma Jean has the power to be Marylyn Monroe.

1. Make others feel special – Some of the world's most powerful communicators understand the importance of making other people feel special. They earn a loyal following based on their ability to make others feel valued, cherished and great about themselves. Charismatic communicators know how to hold a compelling conversation by concentrating on other people's life, passions, and interests. They demonstrate a genuine interest in people. People seldom forget how you make them feel even if they don't remember what you did or didn't do for them. Use this to your benefit through every given opportunity to make people feel special about them! Speak about their strengths, encourage/hail them publicly, and highlight their positives – basically, place them on a pedestal to increase your own likeability and charisma.

2. Express discomfort or have tough conversations with ease – At times, we have no choice but to have difficult, uncomfortable conversations with people or communicate with difficult people. The manner in which you handle these potentially conflict-laden and tricky situations contribute to our overall popularity. You don't need to go guns and daggers after people if you disagree with them. There can be disagreements and conflicts between people all the time in personal, professional and social settings. However, prevent them from snowballing into something bigger.

When you have something uncomfortable to say to the other person or discuss it with them, say something like, "Jill, I need to speak to you about something that has been troubling me for long. This way you are assuming responsibility for experiencing a particular feeling rather than accusing the other person. When you begin your sentence in the manner mentioned above, the other person immediately lowers his/her defenses and becomes more open and receptive to what you are saying.

Continue with "I don't wish to upset or annoy you. However, if I don't talk about this, I'll stay upset and hurt, which isn't very good, is it? Now, you've already got the other person to agree that stay quiet about the issue is not the best thing to do and that it's healthier to share whatever is troubling you. By presenting this less offensively, you are tackling the issue yet minimizing the scope for conflicts.

The tone should be more non-accusatory and solution based. It reveals you are as much concerned and mindful of other person's emotions, views and ideas as you are about your own.

One technique that works wonderfully well for me when it comes to talking about potentially uncomfortable issues is what I call the sandwich technique! The way it works is – you sandwich or pack a negative statement or remark between two positive statements or remarks to keep in balanced and less offensive.

Let us look at an example. "I think you are a wonderful dancer, your movement and form are very detailed and versatile. However, I'd be happy if you could work on your expressions to accomplish the same level of perfection. You'd be one of the best dancers in our troupe if you manage to do that!" Note what we did here. We placed together a potentially offensive or negative statement (the performer isn't adept at giving the right expressions or has to work on their expressions) between two positive statements to make it acceptable for the listener. The listener will most likely lower his/her defenses and be more accepting of your ideas. Try this method; it is effective across multiple professional interpersonal and social scenarios.

Each time you are about to discuss a seemingly uncomfortable or offensive topic with a person, avoid starting with it straight off the bat. Instead, employ indicators, clues, and signposts. We've all seen signposts on the street that offer us handy clues about where we are headed or the route to our destination. Offer people a heads-up about what's in store for them. Get them mentally prepared before simply dropping the bomb.

Start by saying something to the effect of, "I sincerely want this issue resolved otherwise I wouldn't be talking to you" or "I could honestly do with some reassurance from you which is why I am bringing this up with you." You are giving the person a sense of importance that if the person or issue weren't important enough for you, you wouldn't discuss it. You are speaking about it only because it matters! You are expressing your point in a more nonoffensive and non-accusatory way. The person will end up thinking that the objective of your talk isn't to accuse or frame them but to get reassurance from them, which makes them more open to listening.

3. Adapt to multiple communication styles – This is as important for leaders as for people seeking more harmonious interpersonal relationships. Adapting to different communication styles in integral to the process of a being an effective communicator and speaker. Understand that each person has a unique communication style based on their personality, age, culture and so on. For example, personality A Type people are known to be dominating, obstinate, dynamic and aggressive. To avoid these people from controlling the interaction, you may need to demonstrate more assertiveness and firmness.

Likewise, when you are communicating with baby boomers, you'll use a different communication approach than if you are communicating with Millennials. While baby boomers are more open to personal, face to face communications, Millennials may prefer emails, instant messaging and video conferencing.

As a leader or communicator, you'll be required to tune in to the preferences, personalities, demographics and communication style of your team members or audience. Even in personal encounters, you may have to adapt to your partner's or friend's communication style to build more harmonious and fulfilling relationships.

4. Be a smart observer – Some of the best conversationalists and most effective communicators I know are the ones who notice and talk details. Ever wondered by fiction authors and professional scriptwriters weave such wonderfully imaginative stories, concepts, and ideas? Artists, poets, writers and other creative professionals are brilliant observers. They skillfully notice things and people around them to create ideas, images, and characters. They are pros at observing and absorbing diverse situations while giving it their own interpretation. There is a huge tendency to take in the smallest and most detailed nuances of things around them. They have the tendency to observe more than the average Joe.

These are the people who will offer detailed compliments or comment on a fascinating wall artifact or jewelry piece someone's wearing at a party. They will quickly notice people's accents and start talking to them about it. Their conversations are based on detailed and interesting observations. It comes with practice. Start being more observant and conscious of people and things around you! Give yourself a clear conversation edge by noticing small details that a majority of people overlook. You will come across as an exciting, creative and interesting conversationalist who is in sync with the listener.

Offer interesting, detailed an exciting insight into your conversation. Avoid speaking or talking regarding expected, basic or simplistic. Don't state the obvious. Instead of talking about the latest breaking news that people must've heard a hundred times by now, offer your own unique take or view of it to make the interaction more memorable. Keep some trivia handy or know interesting/fun facts at the back of your hand, and pepper your conversation with it. I also like reading about interesting research in the field of human behavior and psychology, which is almost always a winner. People enjoy talking about psychological research, self-help topics, and behavioral patterns. Pop psychological insights also make for an interesting conversation topic, which appeals to a majority of people.

5. Always offer one or two useful takeaways – Offer people something to take back irrespective of whether you are addressing a single person or a group of people who are struggling with an issue. Always end your talk or conversation with a couple of actionable, practical and realistic takeaways can be applied in their daily life. It will increase the value of your conversations, and make interacting with you more desirable.

Avoid talking to people in a patronizing or sermonizing manner when they share an issue or problem with you. I know plenty of people who talk down to others or imply that they've been really foolish to get into xyz situation. Don't do that. Talking down to people never helps. You'll seldom win people by making them feel miserable about themselves. Instead, empathize with them, and offer practical solutions. Unsolicited opinions and sermons serve no purpose. Give them an actionable piece of advice they can start implementing immediately. At the end of the conversation, they should have a valuable and doable solution.

For instance, let us say someone is a chain smoker and is talking about the challenge of giving up their nicotine addiction. Instead of telling them they should reduce the number of cigarettes smoked per day or adopt a healthier lifestyle, mention a quick, actionable and practical tip such as chewing gum each time they feel the urge to smoke (just an example) or spending coffee breaks away from co-workers who smoke. This makes you appear more solution focused instead of patronizing.

6. Employ the power of personal stories – Charismatic communicators know how to make themselves irresistible, likable and relatable by narrating personal experiences and anecdotes. They make their interactions even more interesting, fascinating and personal by sharing their own stories as examples or to demonstrate to the other person how they've been in a similar situation. It makes them come across as more identifiable and relatable. This technique also helps create a common foundation for establishing deeper and more meaningful relationships with people.

Sir Paul McCartney utilized this technique cleverly to build a rapport with his audience before every live performance. He used to offer a background story, influence or inspiration for a song or behind the scenes take on the song or incidents/anecdotes while the song was made. This added more punch to his performance. Another superb way of transforming into an interesting conversationalist is to use rhetorical questions liberally in your conversation. Are you having a great time? What's next? Do you know the secret for xyz? It keeps the listener hooked by building anticipation.

One tip I picked up from powerful communicators is using contrast to convey their ideas compellingly and persuasively. For instance, a statement such as "we are concerned about the value we offer our customers" can be delivered more convincing using contrast like, "while our competitors/other companies are focused on low prices, we are concerned about offering more value to our customers." Contrast makes what you are trying to express come across as more power-packed. It leaves the listener or audience thinking.

7. Use metaphors – Metaphors make for amazing conversation elements because they stimulate the listener's imagination and create a more vivid picture of what he/she is trying to convey. As a speaker, you can stir the right feelings, emotions, and visuals in people by using metaphors. Do some online research to use metaphors connected with a common conversation topic. Have a ready bank of smart metaphors for common scenarios and ideas Metaphors help simplify complicated issues for the listener and audience. You can put across your point more effectively using powerful metaphors.

8. Confidence is the key factor – Confidence is the most important factor when it comes to wowing people. It doesn't come in a day. You won't go from being a self-conscious and socially inhibited person to a rock star social being overnight. Confidence and self-assuredness don't equal arrogance. It is being comfortable in your skin and having faith in your capabilities. Keep a polite, well-mannered, courteous and assertive stance while communicating with people. Even if you are feeling nervous and anxious from with, avoid coming across as timid, overwhelmed and intimidated.

Focus on your grooming. Confidence comes from how good you feel about yourself. Wear smart, appropriate and well-fitting clothes that flatter your body type. It impacts how you feel about yourself, and carry yourself in front of others. Remember, you have merely 4 seconds to make a positive first impression on people. That's when you haven't even spoken to them. They will form an impression about you most likely based on how you're dressed.

Develop the art of speaking with conviction. If you want to develop greater confidence, stand in the front of the mirror while talking. This helps you realize how you come across to others while talking. You'll also identify areas of improvement to boost overall confidence.

Confidence is a huge component of charisma. Also, it is an evolving trait. It's a work in progress. If something is destroying your confidence or making you feel inadequate about yourself, pin it down. There can be some things from speech to hair to knowledge. Focus on growing your positives, and improving your weaknesses. Boost your personal appearance, skills, posture, and knowledge to make you feel wonderful about yourself.

9. Use humor to your advantage – Ask the next 10-20 people you interact with what makes a person highly irresistible to them, and a majority will most likely respond with a fabulous sense of humor. Who doesn't like people who make them laugh! People with a wonderful sense of humor are attractive, popular and much sought after everywhere. They have people hooked to everything they say and do. There is an unmistakable charisma surrounding them. Ever thought about why Oprah Winfrey is among the wealthiest and most sought-after television/media personalities? She is a wonderful blend of humor, honesty, and empathy (one of the most killer combinations when it comes to winning people).

Impress people with well-timed and smart one-liners. You

can read up some in advance, and use them at the opportune moment. Demonstrating your sense of humor with intelligent jokes and one-liners makes you come across as more self-confident and comfortable in your skin. I know plenty of people who use self-depreciating humor to their advantage. It makes them appear charismatic, self-assured and high on confidence. People who crack the perfect jokes at the perfect time are just much sought after at all social gatherings. Consciously develop a sense of humor if you feel you lack it. Read everything from comic strips to satire.

Watch more stand-up comedies, where skilled comedians slay it with their funny lines. Think about the funniest thing you can say in any situation. Learn to look at the funnier side of things, even if the situation seems challenging in the face of it. A person who can employ humor, even in the gloomiest situation can be irresistible. With all the stress, worries and anxiety filling our lives on a daily basis, people with a sense of humor are like a breath of fresh air.

Make other people laugh, and activate their feel-good hormones. You will always have a solid edge over others if you can make people smile or laugh. Have you observed how you are likely to buy from salespeople who make you laugh? Contrast this with people who simply go on and on about a product's features in a tiring monotone. We all know how men/women with a totally dig-worthy sense of humor have the most attractive girls/boys flocking to them. They are the subject of absolute envy. Start developing a sense of humor today by reading more, watching funny content, and coming up with your own creative lines (think about the most hilarious thing you can say in any situation).

Ensure you respect an individual's threshold, preferences, and taste of humor before going on a joke-cracking spree. Different people have different tastes when it comes to humor. What is funny for one person may be downright offensive to another. You have to keep everyone's preferences and tastes in mind before attempting to make them laugh.

Avoid overdoing the humor by becoming a laugh a minute joke machine. It can get jarred beyond a point of time when people realize you are all fluff and humor, and can't have a serious, meaningful conversation. Balance humor and jokes with serious, insightful discussions. If you crack a joke after appearing serious or making an insightful conversation, you'll appear funnier. Make your sense of humor more qualitative.

10. Be genuine and authentic – This should be understood, but it's funny how many get it completely wrong. They put on pretenses, and come across as highly obnoxious and preposterous to others. Do not pretend to be something you clearly aren't.

While it alright to fake a little confidence to be able to be practice being more at ease in social relationships and develop greater self-assuredness in social situations, don't try to project something you are not just to be popular. Once the mask wears off, people will discover the truth and stay miles away from you. Make a conscious to increase your charisma, become more influential and develop a more persuasive communication style, while still being true to yourself. Stay natural, authentic and trustworthy. You should come across genuine to other people to inspire their trust and increase your likeability factor.

Some of the most popular people I know are completely unpretentious and genuine, while still staying confident and self-assured. They are not afraid of admitting their mistakes. It only makes them more relatable, human, likable and honest. Avoiding wearing a mask of perfection every time. It makes you appear uncool and fake in the long run. Don't be preoccupied with saying or doing the perfect thing at the perfect time. It doesn't help you come across as relatable and reliable.

If something is stopping you from being confident or self-assured in social situations, unveil it yourself instead of worrying about hiding it. Don't allow anything to hold you back or kill your confidence. For example, something as small as a pimple on your face crumpled clothes or messy hair that can make you feel conscious. You feel nervous and conscious because you think others are going to judge you based on it.

If you think something is making you look or feel awkward and is becoming your weakness, masterfully turn it into your strength by resorting to humor. Talk upfront about it rather than having people speak in hushed tones, leading to greater anxiety. Comment humorous about how your hair looks totally windswept or out of the bed look is the next big thing or something similar, so you are able to make others laugh by poking fun at yourself. Take control, and reduce chances of others taking pot shots at your weakness.

When you have already stated up-front that you are terrible at something in a humorous way, you eliminate the chances of others commenting on it. Once it's laughed and done with, slim chances people are going to bring it up again in the conversation or laugh at it all over again. This invariably reduces your stress, anxiety, fear, and nervousness. You will no longer be afraid of people discovering your weaknesses, which will make it easier for you to behold more confident interactions. Also, you'll appear funnier, more interesting, relatable and unpretentious. In a scenario where people are forever putting on an act of trying to be something they clearly aren't, you'll be like a breath of fresh air.

Chapter Four:

Communication Blunders We Make

It isn't just leaders and head honchos who need ace communication skills. Everyone needs it to understand and influence each other. Heck, you need awesome communication skills to persuade your best friend to go for lunch at your favorite café over the others.

Think about a scenario where you are explaining to your team member as a project manager about what he/she's done wrong for 15 long minutes. You've mentioned everything you wanted to, only to realize they aren't listening! Or your CEO is overreacting to a small issue, and you can't muster the courage to tell them that because of the possible consequences. There are plenty of communication blunders we make all the time that hampers our connection with people. The most unfortunate part of these blunders is that at times we can't even pin down the issue to rectify it. We don't know why a person doesn't respond in an intended manner or why we can't get people to do what we want or why they stop listening to us.

Worse, there can be misunderstandings and heated arguments when small issues get blown out of proportion owing to lack of communication.

Here are some of the most common communication mistakes we make that impede the process of effective communication, and prevent us from enjoying healthy, rewarding and fulfilling relationships.

The defense ninja – This is when we stop listening and start attacking people by becoming defensive. Each time a person a says something even remotely critical to us, our lizard brain starts tick-tocking in overdrive mode to become defensive. We believe people are simply trying to put us down even when their criticism is constructive and well-intended. Similarly, if you are dealing with someone who stops listening and starts defending themselves, don't make it sound like you are accusing the person.

Drop their defensive guard by using the sandwich method described earlier by juxtaposing a potentially negative statement between two positives. Also, don't pronounce your statement as if it's the gospel truth. Begin by saying you could be wrong, and that you both should consider and evaluate the facts to gauge if you are right. State up front that you could be wrong. This immediately drops the listener's guard and gets them to be more open and receptive to what you are saying. Instead of making the other person feel responsible for what you are saying, accept responsibility for how you are feeling by using more "I" and less "you." This makes you come across as responsible for feeling or thinking something like it is your own point of view. It sounds less accusatory and offensive to the other person. They won't feel you are accusing, criticizing or blaming them for something, which immediately lowers their defense.

Instead of telling the other person, "you never have enough time for me" or "you don't spend enough time with me" try saying "I'd really love if we could spend more time together because I really love spending time with you" or "I really cherish my time with you. Let's work on spending more time together." In the latter, you are putting across your point without accusing the other person.

Similarly, instead of saying, "stop making fun of me in front of others" you can say, "It hurts my feelings when you make fun of me in front of others." You are accepting responsibility for feeling a certain way rather than accusing the other person.

People stop listening when they get the impression of being attacked. Let us say as a manager of a team, you have to communicate with a team member that they aren't being effective in their role or a specific project. Instead of saying, "You aren't working effectively on this project" or "you are an ineffective team member, now do it the way I tell you" you can say, "I have extensive experience handling projects like these and the way to go about it is............"

This technique works because people are less likely to get defensive when you speak for yourself. They are more accepting, open and receptive to reflect on what you are trying to convey to them, even it isn't very positive.

Again, you minimize the chances of conflict or arguments about whether you are right. Since you mentioned things about yourself, things remain indisputable. On the other hand, if you would've said things about the other person, he/she would most likely have gotten defensive and contested your view. When we speak about ourselves, we shut the chances of another person disputing it.

The never-ending struck record – Some people have the tendency to go on and on until the other person stops listening and responding. I mean there's only so much their brain can actively process before switching off. Long-winded, wordy sentences that go on forever tire people out. Stop rambling and stick to the point if you want to be an effective communicator. Fine tune your messages to make it more power-packed. Use a full-stop after your messages are conveyed for the first time. Give the listener an opportunity to ask questions or offer their own take. This way you get the opportunity to clarify something that wasn't clear right at the onset. To check a person's initial understanding, you can make your point and pose a question.

Avoid rambling about the same things like a stuck record. I observe plenty of communicators around me putting across the same point using different words. They'll reframe their words and sentences to become redundant in the end. If you think the other person hasn't understood what you are trying to say, try meta-communication. This simply means you are commenting on the conversation to get a person to talk. For example, if the listener isn't reacting to an important message, you can say something like, "Hey, I notice that you aren't responding to what I spoke just now. However, I think it is important and relevant to our performance as a team. How come?" This gives you an opportunity to know why the person has switched off or whether they understood what you said. Instead of trying to say the same thing using different words and phrases because you think the person hasn't understood what you are trying to convey, use meta-communication to do a check-in on response and understanding level.

Sugar coating or neutralizing your message – Plenty of leaders communicators make themselves ineffective when they pointlessly neutralize their message by following up a powerful and thoughtful message with fluff. The message is robbed of its efficacy. You start by saying something compelling. This is followed by getting worried about its impact on the listener, which leads you to end it with fluff. For example, you may say, "seriously, I didn't mean to say you are not doing this well, but...." or "I didn't mean to be harsh or anything." It just takes away from the efficiency of what you are trying to communicate.

Neutralizing messages also come in the form of non-verbal gestures such as smiling, shrinking your posture, shrugging and so on. It may not be very obvious, but it reduces the impact of your message at a subconscious level. Influential communicators do not resort to neutralizing their messages. They will convey their point less offensively without undermining the importance of their message. They stand up for what they've said without sugar coating it, and also listen to the other person's response.

Similarly, avoid using a one size fits all approach while interacting with different people. Each person has his/her own personality, expectations, needs and views. Ensure your communication adapts to and addresses these differences wherever possible. For example, you may be training a group of people, with each person having his/her own learning style. Take into consideration these differences in learning styles to make your training as impactful as possible. Some people may benefit from more theoretical reading sessions, while others may prefer a more hands-on, practical approach. An effective communicator is someone who can accommodate multiple learning styles to ensure he/she is understood.

The clairvoyants and mind readers – This is an amusing breed of communicators who never forget to entertain me. Even before you complete your sentence, they'll jump in and finish it for you. They seem to know and understand everything you are trying to tell them. They are ineffective communicators because instead of actively listening to what the other person is saying, they assume they already know it, and switch off. This tendency to assume and think "we know" what the speaker is saying prevents us from listening to them, where we can end up missing important bits of information.

Listen intently to every word spoken by the person, tune in to the tone of their voice, and watch out for their body language to understand the overall message in its right context. Avoid picking out bits and pieces of information, and assuming you've understood them. Follow the message in its entirety by being a more mindful listener without jumping to conclusions or making assumptions.

At times, knowingly or unknowingly, we practice selective listening. Rather than listening to what the other person is intending to convey, we hear only what we want to hear, and end up lending it our own interpretation. For example, when a person says, "I really want you to master this," they may mean exactly what they said that they want you to be a pro at something. However, you may hear it as, "you are terrible at this currently." This is not what they said or meant. They may have meant that they want your competency levels to increase, which isn't the same as you are not good at it right now. Just that you can get better! However, you hear what you want to hear, which is "you suck at this right now." Avoid practicing selective listening if you want to be an effective listener. Don't filter what the other person says to pick isolated words and phrases. Instead, pay attention to what the other person is saying to understand the message (as a whole) more effectively.

Let us take an example of selective listening to understand how it impacts the communication process. Sue had a tough day at a restaurant where she waits tables. She's had a particularly busy night and gets home to see her partner hooked to a television show. He casually asks her how her day at work was, and she takes off on everything that went wrong. For starters, she had to deal with plenty of customers since the restaurant was crowded. Then, she didn't manage to make a lot of money in tips. Sue finishes off with how the last group of customers at the table she was serving, ran up a bill for $400 without leaving behind any tip, though she went out of the way to offer good service.

Her partner doesn't say much and instead begins to laugh. Sue asks him what's so funny when she is fuming. He replies he wasn't laughing at her, but at the hilarious situation in the television show. By now Sue is losing it. He didn't say anything to comfort her, which made Sue question him if he'd even heard a single word of what she said. He went on to say, "it is obvious I did, you should be glad about earning a $400 tip from your last group of customers." Sue picked her stuff and stormed out in anger, banging the door behind her while her partner was left wondering where he'd gone wrong. You see the problem with their interaction? Sue's partner practiced selective listening. He wasn't actively listening to her but engaged in other things that caught his attention.

Even when we commit to fully hearing everything, our lives can be full of selective listening opportunities, where we hear only what we want, while leaving out important information bits. It can come across as mighty rude, inconsiderate and disrespectful to the other person.

The closed mind and prejudice champ – How many times have you come across people who will filter what you are saying through their own biases, prejudices, preconceived notions, and limited beliefs? Doesn't it get your goat or act as a barrier to effective communication? Of course. Everyone has their own values, views, and beliefs. However, being rigid or inflexible in your approach prevents you from learning something new or being open to what the speaker is saying. We operate with pre-held beliefs that stop us from acquiring new insights about a person or situation.

Also, not everyone you come across is going to share your views. Empathy and understanding are the biggest tools for constructive and positive communication. When you empathize with people, you understand where they are coming from even if you disagree with them. The key to developing sound interpersonal skills and effective listening is to keep an open, and accepting mind. Tyr to place yourself in the other's shoes to understand what they think the way they do instead of believing others are always wrong when they disagree with you. Not everyone shares your situation and circumstances. Try and think of things from the perspective of the other person to understand his/her situation more effectively.

The modern world is a melting pot of age groups, abilities, political/worldviews, sexual orientations, ethnicities, cultures, religions and so on. Labeling and categorizing people with sweeping generations can be easy and tempting. However, one of the biggest signs of an effective communicator is developing the art of understanding and considering various viewpoints, even if they do not match ours. Get to know people instead of judging them. Avoid making assumptions unless you have evidence. Making assumptions is the number one enemy of effective listening and communication. You inhibit the process of communication and risk your relationship with the other person by resorting to assumptions and generalizations. It kills the opportunity to get to know and understand the other person.

Make an effort to understand the individual's unique background, life experiences, and personality while listening to them. I'd recommend developing a practice of interacting with new people from places and cultures that are different from yours. Give people space to freely express their views, and take the time to understand these views. Take every person's requirements and expectations into consideration while communicating with them. Be assertive without being disrespectful. Like we saw in an earlier example, even when you disagree with someone, you can say something like, "now that's a different/unique/interesting way of looking at it, which I hadn't considered before. Now I am really curious. Can you elaborate on it? You don't necessarily agree with them, but you are opening the gates for them to share their views, and increase your understanding of why they think what they do. Cultural and social intelligence are nothing but adapting to people from diverse cultures/views/societies to form healthy interpersonal, work and social relationships.

Avoid playing solution provider - If you've read author John Gray's bestseller *Men Are From Mars and Women Are From Venus,* you'll know what I am talking about when I talk about unsolicited solution providers. In the first chapter itself, the author describes how women want someone to simply listen to their outpouring feelings and emotions, while men play Mr. Fix-it all the time trying to find a solution to every problem that's shared with them.

Avoid playing solution provider unless the speaker is actively asking you for advice, suggestion or feedback. Resist the urge to fix things by offering unsolicited advice. A majority of the time when people share their feelings, struggles, and problems, they are not looking for a fix or someone to resolve it for them. They most likely realize that it cannot be resolved, which is why they are so bothered by it. All they need is an empathetic listening ear.

Overcome the urge to offer unwanted or unsolicited suggestions, solution, and advice if you want people to take you seriously or listen to you. Listen to the person attentively, because sometimes all they want is for someone to listen, acknowledge and empathize with their feelings without giving their opinion, advice or suggestions.

Consider this conversation, Person A "The baby is giving me sleepless nights. It is tiring and exhausting."

Person B "You should think about supplementing breastfeeding with bottle feed, so the baby doesn't feel too hungry frequently at night and sleeps with a full tummy."

Did Person A ask Person B for a solution?

Contrast this with, "I understand how tiring and exhausting it can be to handle a newborn baby. It drains one's energy. However, you are doing a wonderful job, and this is just a phase that passes once they grow up. In fact, you'll miss all this once the kid grows up and goes about his/her life independently." You re acknowledging the person's feeling, comforting them, encouraging them, appreciating their efforts and even urging them to make the most of these moments.

The yes-man – You don't have to agree with everything a person is saying to be an effective communicator. This especially true about people who aren't confident, self-assured or have high self-esteem. They are more likely socially awkward and easily intimidated by other people. Even when they don't want to, they'll go with what the other person says without articulating their needs. If you identify with this type, it's time you learn to speak for yourself or take a polite yet firm stand about your needs.

Assertiveness is not the same as aggression. There is a thin line yet the huge difference between the two. Assertiveness is the ability to stand up for yourself while being respectful, polite and non-offensive. You aren't obliged to please everyone every time. It is speaking to people in a balanced, logical and reasonable manner without launching an attack. For instance, "I'd prefer going museum hopping than visiting a club or bar." You aren't issuing orders to the other person like, "We are going museum hopping instead of visiting a club or bar." You are articulating your needs and preferences over issuing orders, which sounds more acceptable to the other person. It is about stating your views or needs in a balanced and genuine manner so everyone can arrive at a win-win situation.

While aggression is mostly about "I win –you lose," assertiveness is about "win-win." The focus is on arriving at a win-win situation rather than having your way. You are mentioning your preferences, but still leaving it open for the other person to give express their views and preferences. When you clarify your and the other person's needs, the chances of arriving at a compromise increase. Say a polite yet firm "no" when you aren't up for something. Gently turn down requests by saying no to the task and not the person.

Assertiveness involves standing up for one's values and being unafraid of expressing your desires, values, needs, and goals of other people. It is about treating people as equals and focusing on mutual respect. You do not intend to hurt, undermine or offend others, just as you won't accept others hurting, undermining or offending you. As an assertive person, you are forever seeking a win-win solution.

Here are some pointers for increasing your assertiveness quotient. View other people as a force you need to work together with, not against. This is true in both interpersonal and professional relationships. The focus should be on collaboration and not competition. View every challenge as an opportunity to connect with people. If there's a potentially challenging situation, see it a wonderful opportunity to leave a positive impression on people by handling the challenge effectively.

When you have an argument or differences with your partner or spouse, you tend to view it as a 'me versus him/her' struggle. Look at it from the perspective that you both are on the same team, and working towards a common resolution instead of "who is right?" This one skill alone will help you build more harmonious and healthy relationships. Be assertive, while focusing on the greater good. Instead of viewing everyone who doesn't agree with you as enemies, see them as allies you need to work with to create a win-win.

Consciously develop the habit of articulating and expressing your needs, preferences, feelings, and views openly. You don't have to go with what everyone is saying. If you have a different take or preferences, make it clear. Do not assume that people will automatically know or realize what you want. One of the top reasons for conflicts within interpersonal, professional and social relationships is people assume others will understand exactly what they want or understand their emotions without them having to say anything. Be honest, precise, clear, polite and respectful while expressing your needs. When you are ordering lunch at a café, would you rather request the waiter to get you a chicken sandwich or ask for chicken on rye with a thick slice of cheddar, tomatoes, lettuce, and cucumber? Why are we afraid of articulating our needs and preferences in our professional, personal and social relationships?

Don't feel guilty or regretful of standing up for yourself. When something doesn't align with your values, beliefs, and priorities, refuse without any over looming guilt. Sometimes, we invariably fill our mind with destructive feelings, guilt, and worries. Learn to replace this guilt with positive self-talk. If you don't loan money to a friend who is constantly living off you without accepting responsibility for his/her life, there is no need to think, "I am a bad person." Instead, say "I deserve to look after my interests, and be financially stable without compromising my financial security."

Another wonderful tip for getting rid of the guilt while staying assertive and saying no to people is to imagine standing up for a loved one. Would you let someone do something similar to a loved one? No right? Now imagine your loved one going through the same. I bet my last penny you won't hesitate to take a stand when it comes to a loved one. Imagine taking a stand for them. It will be much easier to speak for someone you love and care about.

Use statements starting with "I" than "you," where you

accept responsibility for feeling a certain way rather than accusing the other person.

Obsessed with winning – One of the most annoying bunch of people to communicate with is those who think they are born to hijack and win every conversation. Read this twice if you have to, but you are never going to win an argument or get a person to agree with by beginning with, "I will prove you wrong here" or "I am going to prove xyz point to you." You only end up raising people's defenses by revealing how hell-bent you are on proving them wrong.

Avoid arousing people's opposition and defenses. The listener is most likely preparing for a mental battle with you. In effect, you are urging them to get their arms ready. I know a lot of people who will start a topic with, "no that's not true. Let me prove you wrong here." Or "that's untrue. I am going to show you how wrong you are." What's the point in informing a person that you are going to defeat him/her? Do it more logical and thoughtfully. Understand that changing people's mind or views isn't easy. When you establish early on that you are trying to prove something to a person, they'll rarely want to admit they were wrong or that you've proved yourself right.

Do not let anyone know you are attempting to prove them wrong. Do it smartly using facts and logic. Even when you know someone is wrong, go along with them by saying something like, "Well, I was thinking a bit differently about this and I could be wrong. I often am wrong just like anyone else. Let's examine the facts, what should they be?" See what we did there? We are taking a more scientific, neutral and balanced approach. This immediately sheds the other person's defenses.

No sane person on this planet can object to something like, "I can very well be wrong. Let us look at the facts." Think about a scientist's approach. Does he or she go about trying to prove people wrong? They only uncover facts. This should be your approach to arguments if you wish to be an effective communicator. Be more balanced and scientific when dealing with potentially uncomfortable topics.

You won't get into any trouble by admitting you could be wrong. It will prevent the issue from spiraling out of control and will lead the other person to adopt a similar balanced, objective and fair stance. The other person will realize that they can also be wrong. When you strengthen your attack, the other person follows suit. When you drop your defenses by stating you could be incorrect, the other is likely to do the same. Don't tell a person he/she is wrong straight off the bat when you want to prove them wrong.

When people don't face compelling emotions or resistance, they are likely to change their stance. However, when people are straight off told they are incorrect, they did not just resent it, but also work harder to prove themselves correct. This creates an endless loop of arguments, differences, and conflicts. When our self-worth, knowledge or views are threatened, we invariably toughen. Make people drop their guard by stating upfront that you can be wrong.

Chapter Five:

Approaching a Group for Rapport Building

Yes, you can make good friends just about anywhere. Even if you are in an unknown place where you don't know anyone or in a new city! Chatting up with unknown people is a great way to grow your social circle and make new friends. The ability to approach a group already involved in the discussion is a huge plus because this can target many people for interaction at once.

If you are anything like I was in the days when I'd just started working, you are petrified of groups. You find the task of approaching a group highly daunting and intimidating. Being nervous is alright. It requires slightly intermediate or advanced communication skills to be able to earn a breakthrough in a group. However, it isn't impossible. It is pretty doable.

Each time I approached a group, it would feel like I am

entering a den filled with hungry lions. As soon as you walk towards the groups and start speaking, there is a tremendous amount of pressure to say and do the right things. Everyone has their gaze fixed on you, and you better make it worth their while by saying or doing something interesting. Otherwise, you are just another unwanted intrusion.

It is precisely for this reason that people are wary of approaching groups. They will only begin conversations with people appear to be by themselves (much easier). However, this limits your options of connecting with maximum people, making more friends and revamping your social circle. People who've mastered the art of approaching groups smoothly and effortlessly are stars at any party. They will skillfully glide from one group to another. Others can't find the courage to do it until they've downed a couple of drinks. However, you can be a successful communicator who can approach any group with practice and effort wherever you are currently in your social confidence level.

Here are some of the best tips that can help you slay it like a boss when it comes to communicating with a bunch of people you are approaching or meeting for the first time.

Dynamics and Tips for Approaching and Communicating With Groups

I am going to share some of my best secrets that will make

sure that your first few moments of interaction with the group are effortlessly killer. Instead of accumulating a bunch of cold shoulders are icy stares, you'll make more friends.

It is easier to approach a group of people in some places over others. By their nature bars, clubs, cafes, and pubs are easy places to approach a group huddled under one roof to let their hair down and enjoy. Being chatty, interesting and approaching new people here is part of the territory, so people won't really look at you like you've landed straight from Mars if you approach them in any of these places. Start with these places if you are overwhelmed by the idea of approaching groups already engaged in a conversation. The atmosphere is more relaxed, and people more or less expect to be approached by strangers.

Now, there are other places which are may be informal and relaxed, but people aren't exactly squeezed together here. For instance, a tourist favorite beach. These are people are huddled with their own intimate circle pretty much oblivious to people around them.

It's a challenge to communicate with groups where you don't know their purpose for being in a particular place. For example, a group sitting in an isolated park. Are they receptive to a rank stranger infiltrating their intimate gathering? The most awkward part is people seeing and staring at you all the way while you walk up to them, which hampers your ability to approach them smoothly. Leave these for later when you've developed sufficient confidence in approaching people in a more 'watering hole,' friendly type of places where approaching strangers and groups is a norm.

Here are some tips to approach groups like a pro

1. Avoid starting off with a closed-ended question – Once you introduce yourself and initiate conversation with a group that's already involved in a discussion (wait until they finish speaking), don't start off with a closed-ended question. Chances are these strangers who aren't too familiar with you will simply answer the question in a word or two and keep quiet again. Then there's an awkward silence. Since you approached the group in the first place, the onus of picking up the conversation falls back on you. The most likely outcome of asking a closed-ended question is you'll hang around for some time before leaving. Initially, people may answer your question to avoid coming across as impolite. However, eventually, you'll be left with no option but to quit.

Instead, assume responsibility by demonstrating proactiveness right from the beginning. Don't use questions that can be answered in a word or two to begin the conversation. You'll have to fight for conversation after the question is answered. Else, you'll have no business being in it.

The thing is, I wouldn't recommend starting a conversation with a group using a question. People are really receptive to answering questions from strangers. They feel like they aren't obliged to reply to you. Even if they do answer your question, they'll seldom expand on it. You'll be left in a situation where you will look awkward hanging around. Instead, add something of value to the group. Don't take away their time by posing questions. Unless you create more conversations from the question, avoid asking questions. Walk up to the group with something fascinating, exciting and valuable. This makes them more receptive to you.

2. Use the foot in the door strategy I often use while approaching a group. If you are slightly shy and low on confidence while approaching a large group, get your foot in the door by chatting up a person in the group. It's the same strategy we used in high school to make our way into the most popular and coolest gang. To get an entryway into the group, a majority of us would befriend someone from the group. In a bigger group, spot a person who is on the periphery or not in the center of all the action. They appear left out or disinterested in the topic or seem focused elsewhere.

Start by approaching this person, who will most likely be receptive and open to what you are saying. Once you are able to strike a conversation with them, slowly transition your attention toward the group, while speaking to everyone. Ensure that you use this technique only on someone who doesn't appear interested in the group's talk. Don't try to switch the attention of a person who is clearly engaged and participating actively in the group conversation. You can also hold on until a group member is on their own. They may separate from the group to buy a drink or visit the restroom. This is your chance! Start talking when they are alone. Later, join their friends with them. The person will more likely than not introduce you to the group.

When it comes to professional networking or approaching a group of people at a party, gain access to the group gradually and incrementally. Unobtrusively introduce yourself to a person within the group. After a single line introduction, throw in a line about how you'd love to be introduced to the entire group at the right time. The person will more often than not oblige. "I'd really love to be introduced to your co-workers some time if you wouldn't mind."

When the person introduces you to the bigger group, come up with "it's wonderful to meet you all here" and then slip back into listening mode until you are comfortable enough to add value to the conversation. It may take time. In fact, you should take the time to understand the rhythm, flow, and nature of communication within the group. Don't try to jump in with your two cents immediately. Listen, and understand until you are confident of joining back in the conversation. When members of the group disperse or separate, there is a lull in the group conversation. Use this opportunity to strike up a conversation with the remaining group members.

If a group is already engaged in a discussion, wait for people to finish speaking before going up to them and introducing yourself. Follow this up by establishing your objective for approaching the group. For example, Hey, I am John Baker with xyz organization. How are you all? I don't want to interrupt but just wanted to listen to this rather interesting conversation since I caught a few bits of it. More often than not, people won't mind you joining the conversation unless it is something intimate or secretive, in which case you'll be politely told to back off. When it is sufficiently established that people do not want you to be a part of the group interaction, leave gracefully rather than lingering around awkwardly. Find another group that is more open and receptive.

3. The only reason why people seldom approach groups is that they imagine the worst, which is being turned away or rejected in the harshest, most humiliating manner. This isn't the case most of the times, especially if you are approaching them in a courteous, friendly and respectful manner, and not aggressively hitting on them. Generally, at worst, they'll respond in a more non-committal manner and then get back to talking with each other leaving you on the periphery.

Now there are two ways to look at this, you get the message, and move on (which frankly no one on the outside even notices). Then there is another way, which isn't to be confused with when the group is not very open to joining you. Here, the group may be open and accepting of you joining in, but they may not make a lot of effort to involve you in the interaction simply because they expect you to make an effort or initiate yourself into the conversation. You may begin by being the silent person on the outlines. Now if you feel left out of the conversation or rejected, it is more likely your own ideas. The group will be glad to include you in the discussion of you put in more effort.

4. Don't steal anyone's thunder – Do not, I repeat, do not try one-upmanship games in a group to impress people. Avoid stealing another person's thunder if you want to gel effortlessly with the group. Make The mandatory personal introduction with ruffling feathers or sweeping the carpet from some else's feet. Establish your benign intentions, listen, respond and learn. You get a better opportunity to follow-up up with your view and create memorable and meaningful conversation.

5. Consider your position and jump in – Where do you want to position yourself in a group? Give yourself a maximum advantage, so you don't end up hanging on the periphery of the group interaction. According to communication experts, your position in the group largely determines your role in the conversation. If you are seated at the end of a table, you'll most likely feel left out of the conversation. Position yourself in the center to stay in the middle of the group interaction flow. It also subtly reinforced that you are the focal point of the discussion or central to the interaction. Being seated far doesn't make you look like a part of the interaction, which is exactly how it will be.

6. Vary your techniques according to group members – Based on the conversation, the personality of group members, the communication style of the group and so on you will have to vary your communication style. There is no one size fits all when it comes to group communication. Adapt to different groups. Mostly, a large group conversation at an informal event, party or social gathering will be more boisterous. In such a scenario, speaking softly will help you have conversations with yourself, not with others.

Even if you aren't a socially confident person, project a confident persona. Go deep, utilize your diaphragm to the fullest and articulate your words clearly, so you've heard. At times, someone may talk over you when they can't hear you. At times we may not speak with passion and conviction, which gives the other person an opportunity to cut in. Speak loudly, confidently and passionately to be heard.

Some communication experts suggest using a quieter than louder approach, especially at professional gatherings. They believe being quieter helps you get more attention than being louder. People who speak loudly may not communicate with power or authority, thus holding attention. Speak deeply in a low tone which resonates and creates the right impact. Keep your voice low pitched and impactful without demonstrating nervousness. Lower your volume, voice, and tone to express that you have something, which should be heard. Express your ideas with an element of authority. Politely and assertively prevent yourself from being interrupted.

You should be a good listener if you want to be a good group speaker. Know when to be polite, and when you need to strike. Sometimes, the only way to get your foot in the door is by interrupting. Take risks, use different strategies and practice. You won't know what works for certain types of groups and what doesn't until you practice. Use the right timing for interjecting. Keep conversations lighter in the beginning. Apologize when needed. Use humor generously to cleverly disarm other people. If you have a friend or acquaintance in the group, use them to slip your foot in the door.

7. Prepare conversation topics in advance – Before attempting to join a group conversation, do some prior reading to be up to date with current topics and subjects of discussion. Share opinions (keep the topics noncontroversial) and stick to popular topics such as entertainment, health, and sports. Be aware of the latest news that can pop up in the conversation. If something remarkable or important has happened in the day, there's a high chance it's going to be a topic of conversation at any social gathering. Add a brand new perspective or share some unique insights with the group. Personal preferences, experiences, travel, and interests make for interesting group conversation topics.

One of the most important aspects of a group conversation that several people overlook is not being nervous or fearful of silence. In our impatience to establish a quick rapport with everyone, we quit even before other people can process what we spoke. Give people an opportunity to know you, and don't be afraid of some silence. Allow them to understand align with you, and take their time to respond.

Again, when you are asking questions or picking random conversation topics, keep in mind that a group conversation is similar to layers of an onion. Every individual has multiple layers comprising different aspects of their life. Begin peeling off their first layer by sticking to a relatively safe question that they are comfortable answering publicly. This is the initial layer that they are happy to share with others. Then, come up with a follow-up conversation with the initial question. By doing this, you increase the prospect of them going a layer deeper when it comes to sharing about themselves.

When someone shares their problems or challenges by going into deeper layers, avoid trying to fix their problems. Do not give out simplistic solutions, quick-fixes, and advice. If you disagree with someone about an issue, put across your point in a healthy, respectful and empathetic manner. Appear genuinely curious and intrigued by a difference in opinion instead of pouncing on people that yours is the only way to look at it.

Learn to move away from past mistakes. Plenty of people suffer from social anxiety or lack of confidence in social situations owing to a blunder or blunders they made in the past. Evaluate your chances of repeating it. Are there high chances you'll repeat the same mistakes again now that you know better?

You won't make a mockery of yourself each time you approach a group or individual for communication. Learn from past mistakes rather than ruminating over them. Get out of this trap of guilt, regret, shame, and negativity. There's a bright future ahead where your social life is concerned. Go out there and make it happen.

I'll share something wonderful I picked up from a socially awkward friend to move past her regrets and guilt and develop more social confidence. After attending each social gathering or event, she makes a list of the ten best things that happened during the event or gathering. It includes ten new things she's grateful for after each event. Count as many amazing things as you can after attending a social event. It can be a new friend you made at the party or someone you were attracted to and want to date or a potential client you rubbed shoulders with at a gathering or something new you learned by interacting with a person. Gratitude changes your thought frequency from negative to positive in a matter of minutes. It will help you overcome negative feelings of the past and get into a more positive, confident and constructive frame of mind. This, in turn, will help you approach people with greater confidence, self-assuredness, and positivity.

8. Approaching people at conferences – One of the best tips I've picked up for approaching people at conferences and seminars is going up to a person (involved in a group discussion) who asked a good question. Talk to them about the question. It can be a nice icebreaker and a starting point. You can say something like, "I really liked that question you asked the speaker. And I think…" Build a conversation around it with the group. Chances are the person will be more than willing to accommodate you in the group, and even introduce himself/herself and his/her co-workers/associates. Ensure you add value to the conversation or add your own insights. You should be able to add your own interesting and unique two cents to the conversation.

Don't be shy of offering compliments and encouragement to

group members. Everyone loves to have a positive person in their midst. If someone is particularly well-dressed, compliment them for their attire. If someone across as humorous and intelligent, compliment them for their sense of humor. Let people know what you appreciate about them to break the ice, and make them more receptive to what you speak.

This can be another good starting point for a conversation. Avoid over-doing though. A constant flow of compliments may sound insincere. The group may get a feeling that you are simply resorting to flattery to make headway or earn a breakthrough. The key is to keep it limited, sincere and specific. The more specific and detailed your compliments, the more sincere they sound. Instead of simply complimenting them for how wonderful their attire is, you can say something like, "the color compliments your skin tone perfectly" or "I love the color and the cuts on your outfit." Make it specific, so it comes across as a well-observed and thoughtful compliment rather than plain flattery.

9. Request someone to accompany you – A person I knew very closely followed this strategy during the initial days of his social anxiety recovery program (this was an extreme case though). Though he was suffering from acute social anxiety, people with milder social anxiety or plain low social confidence can also benefit from it. The person used to take along a trusted friend or family member to social gatherings during the early stages of his social interaction recovery plan.

If you fear to approach large groups, visiting unknown places or attending big events alone, request someone to accompany you in the beginning. Don't stick to them like Siamese twins and ignore everyone else though. They are just around for support and encouragement, not for you to latch on throughout the event. The idea or thought that someone is around to help you navigate the social situation can give you greater comfort and confidence in talking to strangers. Gradually, you'll learn to be on your own without assistance from others.

Even if you move gradually and slowly, take confident, self-assured steps in the right direction to make progress. You won't transform into a confident social being who is fully equipped to approach groups immediately. However, willpower, consistent effort, and relentless practice will get you there is no time.

Conclusion

Thank you for reading or listening to this book.

I genuinely hope it has offered you multiple techniques, actionable tips, and strategies for being a conversation boss across various settings to enjoy more harmonious, rewarding and fulfilling social, professional and personal relationships.

The objective of the book is to help you get rid of your inhibitions, nervousness, and lack of confidence to take on the world by speaking more confidently and effectively, mastering one skill or strategy at a time until you can speak to just about anyone like a pro. Communication and conversation is the key to building solid, rewarding and lasting relationships along with determining your chances of success in life.

The next step is to start using the actionable techniques mentioned in the book straight away. Information has to be converted into knowledge, which in turn is translated into experience and wisdom. Of course, you won't transform from a nervous and awkward conversationalist or social being into a confident speaker overnight. However, take one step a time to inch closer to your goal. With the application, implementation, and practice, you'll slowly but surely transform into an interesting, engaging and stimulating conversationalist.

Finally, if you enjoyed reading the book, please take the time to share your views by posting a review on Amazon. It'd be highly appreciated!

Made in the USA
Las Vegas, NV
15 May 2021